Animal Masterminds

A CHAPTER BOOK

BY CATHERINE NICHOLS

SCHOLASTIC INC.
New York Toronto London Auckland Sydney
Mexico City New Delhi Hong Kong Buenos Aires

For Joan Kane Nichols,
a great mother, a great writer, and a true mastermind

ACKNOWLEDGMENTS

The author would like to thank all those who gave their time and
knowledge to help with this book. In particular, special thanks go to Dr. Irene
Pepperberg, Associate Professor of Ecology and Evolutionary Biology, University of Arizona;
Dr. Alex Kacelnik, Professor of Behavioral Ecology, Oxford University and
Fellow at the Wissenschaftskolleg zu Berlin; and Dr. Sue Savage-Rumbaugh,
Professor of Biology at Georgia State University.

ISBN 0-516-24460-4

12 11 10 9 8 7 6 5 4 3 2 1   3 4 5 6 7 8/0

Printed in the U.S.A.   61

First Scholastic Book Club printing, September 2003

CONTENTS

INTRODUCTION

How can we tell if an animal is smart or not? One way is to give the animal tests. Scientists call these tests **experiments.**

Every experiment is set up around a question. Can the animal figure out problems? Can it learn quickly? Can it remember what it learned? If the answers are yes, then the animal is probably smart.

All the creatures in this book are animal **masterminds**. Hans the horse was smart enough to go to school. Betty the crow made a hook out of wire and used it to get food. Alex the parrot can tell how objects are the same and how they are different. Panzee the chimp uses a special keyboard to talk to people.

How did these amazing animals get to be so smart? Read their stories and find out.

CHAPTER ONE

CLEVER HANS

Hans was a very **clever** horse. Ask him a question on any subject and Hans could answer it. He knew how to add, subtract, and multiply. He even knew how to tell time. Clever Hans was an amazing horse.

Just how clever was he, though? A German teacher named Wilhelm von Osten bought Hans in 1900. Wilhelm believed that animals were just as smart as

Wilhelm von Osten bought Hans in 1900.

people. To prove this, he gave his horse lessons in spelling, math, history, and music.

Then Wilhelm had people ask his horse questions. If the answer was "yes," Hans would nod. If the answer was "no," he would shake his head. To answer a math question, Hans would tap his hoof. Hans was always right.

Many **scientists** could not believe that a horse was so smart. They thought Wilhelm was somehow giving the horse the answers. So Wilhelm left the room. Hans still got the answers right. Everyone agreed that Clever Hans was very clever.

Almost everyone agreed. One scientist wasn't so sure. He had noticed something. The people asking Hans the questions knew the answers. What would happen if the person didn't know an answer? Hans failed that test. If the questioner didn't know the answer, neither did Hans. So how did Hans fool all those scientists?

Hans was picking up **cues,** or hints, that told him the answer. When people asked their questions, they might raise an eyebrow or nod their heads or hold their breath. These hints told Hans which way to turn his head or when to stop tapping.

Clever Hans performs for a crowd.

$$3 - 2 = 1 \checkmark$$
$$5 - 3 = 2 \checkmark$$
$$5 + 9 = 14 \checkmark$$
$$9 - 6 = 3 \checkmark$$
$$5 + 6 = 11 \checkmark$$
$$5 + 4 = 9 \checkmark$$

Today, scientists remember Clever Hans when they set up their experiments. They want to make sure that the animals can't get cues from the person who gives the test.

In the end, Clever Hans was still clever. He was smart enough to figure out those cues, after all! He just wasn't clever in the way his owner had hoped.

This trainer is wearing dark glasses so the dolphin cannot see her eyes.

CHAPTER TWO

ALEX, ONE SMART PARROT

Alex was in front of the computer. Flying saucers were on the screen. Alex's teacher asked him how many flying saucers there were. "Four," Alex answered. Counting to four may not seem like a big deal, but it is, if you're a parrot.

Alex's teacher is Irene Pepperberg. Irene bought Alex at a pet store in 1977. He was about a year old. Since then, Irene has been training Alex how to **communicate** (kuh-MYOO-nuh-kate) with people.

Alex is an **African gray parrot.** In the wild, parrots live together in groups. They communicate with each other by using their voices. Young parrots learn sounds by **imitating** their parents and other parrots.

Parrots in the wild

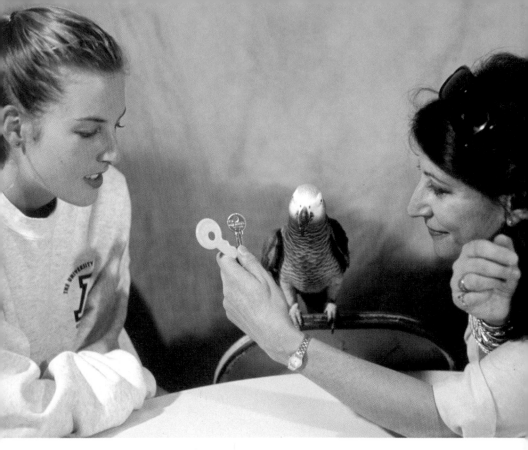

Irene and her helper teach Alex the names of objects.

Irene takes the place of Alex's parents. She teaches him the way they would. Irene also cuddles and plays with Alex. If Alex didn't like his teacher, he would never **cooperate** (koh-OP-uh-rate).

So far, Irene has taught Alex the names of over fifty objects. First, Irene shows Alex the object and lets him hold it. Then she asks her helper to name the object.

Alex listens as the helper says the word. Then it's Alex's turn. After Alex names an object correctly, he is allowed to hold it again. This is his **reward.**

If Alex wants an object, he has to ask for it. Sometimes he'll ask for corn or his favorite treat, cashews. However, Alex does not like to be tricked. If he asks for a walnut, he won't take a banana instead.

Alex does not like to be tricked.

Alex knows many colors, shapes, and numbers. Show him a tray that has six green blocks, five green balls, three red balls, and four red blocks. He will tell you how many blocks are red and how many balls are green.

Alex can **compare** objects, too. He can say how they are different and how they are the same. Show Alex a blue key and a blue cork and ask him how they are the same. Alex will answer, "Color." Show Alex two green beads that are exactly alike and ask how they are different. He will answer, "None."

Alex is allowed to hold an object he names correctly.

Alex can compare objects.

Irene and her helpers work with Alex for eight hours every day. Sometimes Alex gets bored with his lessons. Then he might squawk, "No," and climb down off his perch. Other times, Alex will give the wrong answer, even though he knows the right one.

Once, Alex had to name an object that was green. There were six objects on the tray. Alex named the five objects that were not green. Then he tipped over the tray. Clearly, Alex was saying he'd had enough tests for one day!

Alex has had enough!

CHAPTER THREE

BETTY MAKES A TOOL

Do you know Aesop's fable about the crow and the pitcher? A thirsty crow spotted water at the bottom of a tall pitcher. The crow couldn't reach the water.

Then the crow saw a heap of pebbles. It took a pebble in its beak and dropped it into the pitcher. It dropped pebble after pebble until the water rose high enough for the crow to drink.

THE CROW & THE PITCHER

HOW the cunning old
    Crow got his drink
When 'twas low in the
        pitcher, just think!
Don't say that he spilled it!
With pebbles he filled it,
'Till the water rose up to
            the brink.

· USE · YOUR · WITS ·

THE · EAGLE · AND · THE · CROW

THE Eagle flew off with a lamb;
  Then the Crow thought to lift an old ram,
    In his eaglish conceit,
      The wool tangled his feet,
And the shepherd laid hold of the sham.

: BEWARE · OF · OVERRATING · YOUR · OWN · POWERS :

A page from *Aesop's Fables*

Crows are great problem-solvers, as the story shows. It also shows something else about crows. They are successful at using **tools**. In the story, the crow used pebbles as a tool. The pebbles raised the water level.

Are crows really this smart? Some crows in Japan are animal masterminds. Crows like to eat walnuts. Walnut shells are hard to open, though. The Japanese crows don't let this stop them. They place walnuts at crosswalks when the traffic lights are red.

When the lights turn green, the cars crack open the walnut shells. The smart birds wait until the lights turn red again. Then, they eat the walnuts.

Betty

A crow in England is especially smart. She not only uses tools, she makes them. Who is this unusual bird? Her name is Betty. She is one of two crows tested in an experiment. The scientist in charge of the experiment was Alex Kacelnik.

Alex Kacelnik

Alex put a small bucket filled with food inside a tube. Then he gave two crows, Betty and another crow named Abel, a choice between two kinds of wire. One wire was straight. The other wire was hooked. To get the food, the bucket had to be lifted from the tube. Which piece of wire would the crows choose?

Betty took the hook, but Abel, the older and stronger crow, snatched it away. While Abel played with the hooked wire, Betty tried to get the food using the straight wire. She wasn't able to raise the bucket, though.

Betty was not about to go hungry. She pushed the wire against a tray and bent it. Now the tip of the wire was shaped like a hook. Betty used her new tool to pull up her dinner.

Betty was smart enough to bend wire into a hook to get her food.

A chimpanzee digs for termites.

Crows are not the only animals that use tools. **Chimpanzees** use sticks to dig termites out of their nests.

Orangutans, a kind of ape, also use sticks as tools. A hungry orangutan will push a stick into a beehive and move it around. Then the ape will pull out the stick and suck off the sweet honey.

Sea otters use tools, too. They like to eat **abalone** (ab-uh-LOH-nee), a sea snail with a hard shell. Sea otters use stones to crack open the shells. Then they pop the abalone into their mouths.

A sea otter uses a rock to crack the shell of a clam.

The first time Betty made the hook, Alex was amazed. In the wild, some crows use twigs to get at insects in tree holes. However, crows don't know about wire. A crow had never made its own hook. Alex tested Betty again. He wanted to make sure Betty knew what she was doing. Nine times out of ten Betty made a hook with the wire.

She didn't bend the wire the same way each time. Sometimes she bent it the way she had done the first time. Sometimes she'd stand on the wire and bend it with her beak. If the hook didn't work, she'd work on it until it did.

Betty showed that she's no birdbrain. In fact, she is one smart crow.

CHAPTER FOUR

TALKING CHIMPS

Jane Goodall was walking in a forest in Africa. She saw a chimpanzee on the path. The chimp saw Jane. "Wraaah," the chimp called. The chimp was saying something, but what? Just then, more chimps came out of the forest.

Jane is a scientist. She has studied chimps in the wild for many years. She knew what to do about the chimps. She stayed still. When the chimps saw that Jane wasn't dangerous, they left her alone.

Chimps in the wild communicate with each other in many ways. That was what the chimp in the forest was doing. He was telling other chimps that Jane might be dangerous. The other chimps understood his call. They came to help their friend.

Wild chimps can make about fifty calls. Each call means something different.

Jane Goodall in the forest

Wild chimps can make about fifty calls.

Chimps use gestures to communicate.

Some calls let other chimps know where to find food. Other calls warn chimps about danger.

Chimps also communicate through **gestures** (JESS-churs) and body movements. A chimp who wants to show others who is boss will stand tall. A chimp who is afraid might grin or make a face.

Because chimpanzees communicate so well, some scientists thought they might be able to learn how to talk. In 1947, Keith and Catherine Hayes brought Viki, a baby chimp, into their home. Keith and Catherine treated Viki like a human baby.

They tried to teach her how to speak. After three years, Viki could say four words. She could say *Mama, Papa, up,* and *cup.*

Viki did not say these words clearly, however. She spoke in a rough whisper. Most people could not understand her. It looked like the experiment of teaching a chimp to speak had failed. Why was this?

A chimpanzee's **vocal cords** are different from ours. This makes it impossible for chimps to say the vowels *a, i,* and *u.* Chimps also can't move their tongues as easily as we can.

Scientist Allen Gardner knew that chimps were smart. He knew they were good at using their hands. Instead of teaching chimps to speak, Allen decided he would teach them to use **American Sign Language** (sine LANG-gwij), or **ASL**.

People and chimpanzees have different vocal cords.

Deaf people use their hands to sign words.

ASL is the language used by deaf people. Instead of using their voices to speak, deaf people use their hands to sign.

Washoe was ten-months-old when she came to live with Allen and his wife, Beatrice. Like Viki, Washoe was treated like a human baby.

Washoe had many signs to learn. Allen and Beatrice hired helpers to train Washoe. Roger Fouts was Washoe's favorite helper.

Roger and the other helpers signed to Washoe all the time. They signed to Washoe when she was eating. They signed to her when she was taking her bath. They signed to her when she was getting dressed. After four years, Washoe knew more than 130 signs.

Sometimes, Washoe didn't know the name for an object. Then she did what human babies do. She made up her own sign. For example, one day Washoe and Roger saw a swan in a lake. Washoe had never seen a swan. "WHAT IS THAT?" Roger signed. Washoe looked and then signed back, "WATER BIRD." By putting together two signs she knew, Washoe had made a new sign.

Washoe's "water bird"

Washoe has made up other signs, too. Her sign for celery is PIPE FOOD. What do you think she means when she makes the sign for CANDY DRINK?

Not all scientists agreed that Washoe was using **language** (LANG-gwij). Some of them thought that she was imitating her teachers. They did not think Washoe really understood what she was signing.

Scientist Sue Savage-Rumbaugh has decided to test chimps another way. She has her chimps use a keyboard to communicate. The keyboard has many different **symbols** (SIM-buhls) on it. Each symbol stands for something. For instance, the symbol of a circle might stand for the word *ball*.

Sue Savage-Rumbaugh with Kanzi

When the chimps want to communicate, they point to the symbols on the keyboard.

Sue uses **bonobos,** a kind of chimp, in her experiments. Sue and her student helpers were trying to teach Matata, a bonobo, how to communicate. A young bonobo named Kanzi was always around when Matata was having her lessons. Sue and her helpers didn't pay attention to Kanzi. One day, the scientists were talking about lights. Kanzi ran over and turned on the light switch. Kanzi had understood them!

Sue tested Kanzi. She discovered that he understood more than 150 spoken words. No one had taught him. He picked up the words the same way a child would. He watched people and listened to what they said.

Sue decided to teach Kanzi the keyboard. Kanzi was a fast learner. By the time he was six, he knew 200 symbols. Today, he is learning how to put together simple sentences.

Sue wanted to find out if only bonobos were good at language. She raised a bonobo named Panbanisha with a common chimp named Panzee. The two young animals spent a lot of time with Kanzi. They watched as Kanzi communicated using the keyboard. Both Panbanisha and Panzee learned how to use the keyboard without any special training. What did this experiment show scientists? Chimps learn language best when they can pick it up on their own, the way young children do.

Kanzi continues to surprise scientists. One day, Sue noticed that he was making

Panzee using the keyboard

quiet noises. Sue and another scientist looked at tapes they had made of Kanzi. They found out that Kanzi made certain sounds at certain times. These sounds seem to stand for words. One sound seems to mean *banana*. The other sounds seem to stand for the words *grapes, juice,* and *yes*. Kanzi hadn't been taught to make these sounds. He was making them on his own.

Can Kanzi talk? Scientists are not sure. They are still testing him. In 1947, scientists tried to teach Viki our language. Today, maybe Kanzi is trying to teach us his.

GLOSSARY

abalone (ab-uh-LOH-nee) a large snail that lives in the sea

African gray parrot a parrot from Africa

American Sign Language (ASL) a language of hand signs used by deaf people to communicate

bonobo a small kind of chimpanzee

chimpanzee a small ape from Africa

clever quick to learn things

communicate (kuh-MYOO-nuh-kate) to share your feelings and thoughts with someone

compare to show how things are alike

cooperate (koh-OP-uh-rate) to work together

cue a hint or signal

experiment a test in order to find out something

gesture (JESS-chur) a hand or body movement that shows meaning

imitate to copy how someone acts

language (LANG-gwij) communication that uses speech or written words

mastermind someone who plans and carries out a project

orangutan a large ape from Southeast Asia

reward a prize for doing something well

scientist a person who studies the natural world

symbol (SIM-buhl) something that stands for something else

tool something that is used to get a job done

vocal cords folds at the top of the windpipe that let a person or animal make sounds

FIND OUT MORE

Clever Hans
www.pbs.org/wnet/nature/animalmind
What goes on inside the animal mind? This website will
tell you.

Alex, One Smart Parrot
www.pbs.org/saf/1201/video/watchonline.htm
Watch a video and see Alex in action. Irene asks Alex
questions and Alex answers them.

Betty Makes a Tool
www.zeebyrd.com/corvi29
Crows are thought to be the smartest of all birds. Learn
more about these interesting animals.

Talking Chimps
www.cwu.edu/~cwuchci/main.html
What does Washoe like to eat? Find out when you visit this
website. You can also watch Washoe and her friends play
on Chimp Cam.

INDEX

PHOTO CREDITS

MEET THE AUTHOR

 Catherine Nichols lives in Jersey City, New Jersey. She has worked in children's publishing as an editor, project manager, and author. She has written many children's books, including several on animals and animal behavior. When she isn't writing, Catherine enjoys playing with her pug, Pablo. While Pablo has never had his intelligence tested, Catherine is sure that he's an animal mastermind. He always seems to know where his treats are hidden!